GET THIS!
THE ANSWER TO LIFE'S FINAL EXAM

Ned Erickson

Whitecaps Media
Houston, Texas
whitecapsmedia.com

Get This!
© 2015 Ned Erickson
All rights reserved

ISBN: 978-1-942732-01-3

Unless otherwise noted, Scripture quotations are from the ESV® Bible (*The Holy Bible, English Standard Version®*), copyright © 2001 by Crossway Bibles, a publishing ministry of Good News Publishers. Used by permission. All rights reserved

Scripture quotations marked "NIV 1984" are taken from the Holy Bible, New International Version®. NIV®. Copyright © 1973, 1978, 1984 by Biblica, Inc. Used by permission of Zondervan. All rights reserved worldwide

Scripture quotations from THE MESSAGE. Copyright © by Eugene H. Peterson 1993, 1994, 1995, 1996, 2000, 2001, 2002. Used by permission of Tyndale House Publishers, Inc.

For information on bulk purchases of this book, please visit whitecapsmedia.com

Printed in the United States of America

Table of Contents

INTRODUCTION		5
STUDY 1	Why God Needs Jesus	9
STUDY 2	Mountains, Masks, & Messes	18
STUDY 3	Paratrooper Jesus	28
STUDY 4	All-In	39
STUDY 5	The Answer to Life's Final Exam	49
STUDY 6	The Get-To-Life	60

Download the Study Guide
for this book at
whitecapsmedia.com

Introduction

Cheat Sheet

I remember the first time I cheated in school. It was on a spelling test. The word was *use*. I wrote out Y-O-U-S (which technically is a word where I come from. Like: "Hey, what are yous guys doing over there?"). But that morning there was something about the way Y-O-U-S looked on the paper that caused my eyes to stray over to Phil's. He had written U-S-E, which didn't look right either. Where was the Y? *Use* sure sounded like it needed a Y. Well Y or no Y, for whatever reason I decided to trust Phil's answer over my own. I carefully erased Y-O-U-S and replaced it with U-S-E and the rest is history.

That day, I learned a valuable lesson: cheating works. If you don't know the answer, look at someone who looks like they do and copy them. For better *and* worse that pretty much defines my growing up.

When I went on the staff of Young Life, a ministry to high school students, there was this guy who looked to me like he had the answers. Believe it or not, he had the same name as my school friend, except he spelled his with an F instead of a P-H. Fil was older than me. I didn't know how much older, but he talked really slow and soothing, which isn't necessarily a sign of old age, but it was something I noticed about him. I knew he was older because, well, one, he was in charge of our group; and two, he dressed like a dad. Anyway, over the course of our three weeks together I pretty much decided that I wanted to be just like him.

As it turned out Fil lived only thirty minutes from where I was going on Young Life staff. Learning that, I decided then and there I was going to make Fil teach me everything he knew. I began to stalk him. Not exactly stalk him. More like I refused to let him out of my sight until he agreed to meet with me. I guess that is stalking. Well, whatever it was, it worked.

Seventeen years later we're still getting together. However, it didn't take me that long to discover Fil didn't have all the answers. Instead, he gave me something even better. He introduced me to the Jesus he knows.

Fil's Jesus is a guy who does whatever it takes to show us how much we are loved. You might think a guy like that would be mushy and sentimental, but what I've come to discover is the word *badass* fits more closely to the Jesus Fil knows. Jim Rayburn, the founder of Young Life, put it this way: "Christ is the strongest, grandest, most attractive personality ever to grace the earth."[1] And over the last twenty years of getting to know Him personally (Jesus, not Jim Rayburn), I'm convinced Rayburn was right. I'm also convinced Jesus graced this earth to give us the answers to life's deepest questions: Who am I? Why am I here? What's the point of it all? But not only that, Jesus came in order to make the answers possible. We'll talk about that later.

For right now, what you need to know is this: There are answers to these questions. In fact, there are also questions *you* need to answer. *Get this: At the end of your life there will be a final exam.* We're all going to take it. You, me, even Charlie over there. And guess what: There's no extra credit. No make-up work. And I don't want to scare you, but the stakes are big. Your eternal fate depends on how you do on this test. That's right. Heaven or hell hinges on the results.

Why am I telling you this? Because this book not only talks about what's on the exam, it's going to give you the answers! That's what this book is: everything you need to know to pass life's final exam. And in the process, you might end up like me, falling in love with the Jesus I know.

Actually, that's the secret: knowing Jesus. But we'll get to that. First, we need to understand why He's so important. So friends, are you ready? Well, ready or not, it's time to make sure those thinking caps are secure—because you and I are about to go to school.

---

[1] Jim Rayburn, *The Diaries of Jim Rayburn* (Morningstar Press and Whitecaps Media, 2008), xvii. The quote continues: "Christ is the strongest, grandest, most attractive personality ever to grace the earth. But a careless messenger with the wrong method can reduce all this magnificence to the level of boredom ... it is a sin to bore anyone with the gospel."

Study 1

Why God Needs Jesus

Did you know that while you are reading this you are spinning 1,000 miles per hour around a planet that is traveling 66,000 miles per hour around a sun that is clipping away at 43,000 miles an hour in a galaxy which is flying through the universe at 483,000 miles per hour?[1] Oh, by the way, that galaxy we live in that is flying through the universe 483,000 miles per hour, it's spinning around a black hole 4 million times the size of our sun. Dizzy yet?

When you think about it, you and I are small. I mean we are really, really, *really* tiny. Consider this: 1.3 million Earths could fit inside the sun, which is just a medium-sized star that is but one star among the 200 billion that make up the Milky Way Galaxy, a galaxy which is but one galaxy among the 100 billion galaxies in the "observable universe." Feeling small? Did you know that the Milky Way is 100,000 light-years across? In other words, if you could travel as fast as light, it would take you 100,000 years to go from one end to the other! And considering that light travels 5.8 *trillion* miles in a single year, that's big!

This is how King David in the Bible put it: "When I look at your heavens, the work of your fingers, the moon and the stars, which you have set in place, what is man that you are mindful of him?"[2] Good question. If the universe was just made for us, it's a little big, wouldn't you say? Well, the truth is God did not create the universe for us. He made it *for Himself.* Let that sink in for a second. Whether we act like it or not, you and I are not the center of the universe. We are not even the center of our galaxy! If all of history was a beach, we would not even be a grain of sand.

Now, here is where it gets crazy, because however small and insignificant you might feel at this moment, you matter a whole lot to God. In fact, you matter so much to Him that He is unwilling to let anything get in the way of you knowing it. So what does God exactly want us to know? In a word, *Himself*. God wants us to know Him, like personally.

But there's a problem. There's a few, actually, but I've already hinted at one: His size. Isaiah 40:12 says that

God can measure the whole universe in the span of His hand. That's right, God is so big the universe can fit between His thumb and pinky finger! In point of comparison, God's hand is to us as we are to a quark. What is a quark you ask? Well, quarks are the particles that make up the nuclei in atoms, and there are more in your body than there are stars in the sky. Now, imagine having a *personal relationship* with one of them. Good luck. Perhaps, now you can see the challenge God faces in having a personal relationship with us. (And it's a little bit bigger than the one I had trying to kiss Wendy, my prom date, who was three inches taller than me, but that's another story.)

Fortunately, God hasn't left us completely in the dark. There are things we can figure out about Him. For instance, we can know by looking up at the stars on a clear night that God is *big*. And we can study the forces of nature and come to the conclusion that God is *powerful*. Scientists theorize that the force of the Big Bang was equivalent to 9.5×10^{53} megatons of TNT.[3] Powerful? I'd say. I'd also say that the study of science and mathematics has clearly demonstrated that God *knows what He's doing*. There are "laws" (like gravity) that govern everything that happens in the universe, and in order for you and me to even exist, all those laws must work exactly the way they're designed. Think about it: If gravity, for example, decided to disobey for just ten seconds, it would be over for you and me. This universe certainly appears like a well-oiled machine.

Here on earth, we can know things about God as well. Like, we can take a deep breath and figure out that God *provides for us what we need to live*. We can look at something as ordinary as fungi (recent estimates place the total number of fungi species on earth at 5.1 million)[4] and tell that God is *creative*. And we can deduce that God *has a sense of humor* by observing animals like the platypus, or guess that God *likes beautiful things* by gazing at a flower, or even into a mirror.

But there is something about God that we cannot know by studying the universe or even looking in the mirror, and it happens to be the most important thing about Him. What is it, you ask? It's this: *love*.

God is love. Love is not God, but of all the words to describe what God is like, *love* is the best. Did you get that? *The most important character trait of God is not that He's big, powerful, smart, or creative (though all those things are true), it's love.*

God loves what He creates. And God created you. So by the transitive property (a law God also created) *God loves you.* John 3:16 says, "For God so loved the world, that he gave his only Son, that whoever believes in him should not perish but have eternal life." We'll unpack the second part of this verse later (it has to do with the final exam); right now, let's focus on the first part.

Get this: For as long as we have been around and for reasons we may never fully understand, God has loved us. But as we already mentioned, He has this size problem. So God did something incredible. *He sent His Son Jesus.* You may have heard that before. Maybe you've heard it so many times it's lost a little of its incredibleness. But think about it. God—the Creator, the One whose hand is as big as the universe—became a person.

This is the way the book of Hebrews explains it: Jesus "is the radiance of the glory of God and the exact imprint of his nature."[5] The writer here uses a metaphor. Just like the sun sends light (literally its *radiation* through light particles) to earth, God sent His Son, Jesus. In other words, the sun doesn't stay up in the sky; it comes to earth and gives us light. In fact, we *personally experience* the sun through the light that hits our skin and gives us sunburns or the light that helps the plants we eat grow or the light that enters our eyes and allows us to see.

The same is true with Jesus. He came to earth *so that we could see.* Without light, there would only be darkness and, get this: no light, *no life*. Life doesn't exist without light. And just like real light, there's no life without Jesus. Like the sun, Jesus came to give us life!

Let's keep going with the sun analogy. Even though the sun is 93 million miles away from Earth, we have a personal knowledge of the sun because particles of actual sun left the heavens and came to Earth. Did you get it? Real sun is hitting you right now. Of course, no analogy is perfect; God isn't 93 million miles away. He's as much here as He is there. And it's not like there are gajillions of Jesuses—the world needed only one. But this much is true: Jesus is God, just like the sun rays that hit our skin are sun. There is no difference.

Jesus is the *exact imprint, or representation,* of God.

Why is this important? Because if it's true, then everything we know about Jesus is true about God. How do we know God loves us? God sent His Son, and as it says in Romans, "God shows his love for us in that while we were still sinners, Christ died for us."[6] Jesus Himself said: "Greater love has no one than this, that someone lay down his life for his friends."[7] Another way to put it, Jesus shows us the heart of God.

Now, this is equally important to understand: Anything that is *not* true about Jesus is false about God. So if you thought that God hates fun, how do you explain that Jesus' first miracle was at a party? Why did Jesus choose to associate with "sinners"? Why did prostitutes love Him and religious people want Him dead? What Jesus actually shows us is that not only did God create life, He wants us to *live it fully*! One of the most often quoted sayings of Jesus is, "I came that they may have life, and have it abundantly."[8]

Jesus is the only way we know the whole truth about God.

The great thinker and writer Brennan Manning put it this way:

> Jesus alone reveals who God is ... We cannot deduce anything about Jesus from what we think we know about God; however, we must deduce everything about God from what we know about Jesus. This implies that all of our prevailing images and understandings of God must crumble in the earthquake of Jesus' self-disclosure.[9]

To sum up, God is awesome, so He sent His Son Jesus to make sure the world knew just how awesome He is.

Think about it, if God had not sent His Son, we would have no idea that He loves us, or wants a personal relationship with us, or cares about us at all. Without Jesus, how could we know we could be forgiven? How would we figure out that God has the power to heal our brokenness or understands what we're going through? How would we know that He longs for us to live with Him forever? "Long ago, at many times and in many ways, God spoke to our fathers by the prophets, but in these last days he has spoken to us by his Son" (Hebrews 1:1–2).

Without Jesus, we'd just be guessing. E. Stanley Jones observed,

> What we find in our upward search for God is not God, but our projection of our thoughts into the heavens and calling it God ... We create God in the image of our imagination. And this is "no true image." Apart from Jesus we know little or nothing about God.[10]

Sure, we could know God is big without Jesus. But what could we know of His heart? How could we know that He could bring the dead back to life? Only by Jesus do we know this. In Jesus, God solved not only His size problem, but also His invisibility problem as well since we know from the Old Testament that if you did catch a glimpse of God you'd immediately fall down dead. A problem, wouldn't you say? (There's another problem, but we'll get to it in the next study.)

For right now, let's focus on this. God needed Jesus in order to reveal His true nature. In His Son, God became visible, touchable, and *real*. Not only that, Jesus also gave us a way to see the world, each other, and ourselves the way God really does—in other words, as we truly are.

---

[1] Andrew Fraknoi, "How Fast Are You Moving When You Are Sitting Still?" (Foothill College and the Astronomical Society of the Pacific); retrieved at http://www.astrosociety.org/edu/publications/tnl/71/uitc071.pdf.

[2] Psalm 8:3–4.

[3] Found at http://imagine.gsfc.nasa.gov/docs/ask_astro/answers/980211b.html.

[4] Meredith Blackwell, "The Fungi: 1,2,3 … 5.1 million species?", American Journal of Botany, August 19, 2011; retreived at http://www.amjbot.org/content/98/3/426.full.

[5] Hebrews 1:3.

[6] Romans 5:8.

[7] John 15:13.

[8] John 10:10.

[9] Brennan Manning, *Ruthless Trust* (New York, New York; Harper Collins, 2009), 88.

[10] E. Stanley Jones, *The Word Became Flesh* (Nashville, Tennessee; Abingdon Press, 2006), 24.

Study 2

Mountains, Masks, and Messes

There are fifty-four mountains in Colorado that are over fourteen thousand feet tall. "Fourteeners" they're called. Catchy name. Creative. Well, when my wife Lia, our dog, and I moved to Colorado I had this crazy idea to climb every one.

The thought captivated my imagination. Maybe it was the call of the wild, the physical challenge. For whatever reason, the allure of the mountains was irresistible to me. I bought books. I memorized maps. I learned how to make GORP. I was seriously all-in.

And so, early one clear June morning, my red Saturn crawled up this 4-wheel drive "road," careened around one hairpin turn then another, nearly ran over a herd of bighorn sheep, crossed over a raging creek about three inches deep and finally parked in what could have passed for a Hollywood moonscape. Five hours later, I had "bagged" my first peak: Mount Bierstadt. Elevation 14,065 feet. An "easy" mountain, so they say. It kicked my butt.

The second "easiest" fourteener was a peak called Mount Sherman. The trail guide described it as a short approach followed by a long gentle on-ramp leading to a summit that was so flat and wide an airplane once landed on it. Sounded good to me. Once again, I woke up early and coaxed my red Saturn to what felt like the nether reaches. I was glad to see a Chevy Trailblazer parked off to the side. Pulling in behind it, I started hiking. Ten minutes in, I saw the Chevy Trailblazers ahead of me. "Sweet," I said to myself. "I'll just follow them to the top."

Thirty minutes later, I caught up to them. We exchanged pleasantries. I commented how I had recently climbed Mount Bierstadt and was hoping to bag this one before lunch. As hoped, they reacted with awe and wonder. I offered them some homemade GORP. They passed on it. I took the lead. Not a little impressed with myself, I'd glance back every once in a while at the ever-increasing distance between the Chevy Trailblazers and me. Finally, the summit was in sight. A short, exhausting scramble later, I was on top, pumping my arms over my head like Rocky.

It was then I noticed it. The mountain directly next to the mountain I was standing on was taller. "That's weird," I thought. Looking down, I saw this odd-shaped canister on the ground. I found out later such canisters contain logbooks where people record their summit experiences. I untwisted the cap and read the first entry. It was written three weeks previously. It said: "We never thought we'd reach the top of Mount Sheridan, but here we are!" *WHAT!? Mount Sheridan! What happened to Mount Sherman? Are you telling me I just climbed the wrong mountain?* Not only that, but it turned out that Mount Sheridan, at a "mere" 13,748 feet wasn't even a "fourteener." Off in the distance, I watched the Chevy Trailblazers slogging it up the gentle on-ramp of the peak that was taller than the one I was standing on. All I could do was walk back down and start over, several hours of hiking, wasted.

I doubt that at any point during your life you decided, "Hey, I'm going to choose the wrong path." Most of us, most of the time, make decisions based on what we believe will work out best for us. Unfortunately, and you know this from experience, what we *think* is the best is not always *the best*. In fact, more than likely you have already made a complete mess of things and gotten yourself so off-target you have no clue how to find the right path.

Isaiah 53:6 says: "All we like sheep have gone astray; we have turned—every one—to his own way." In other words, you might not have strayed to the top of Mount Sheridan, but you have strayed somewhere. This is probably not news to you. If you are anything like me, you are one royal mess on the inside. Now, on the outside, it may not appear that way. The School You might get top grades. The Church You might look squeaky clean. The You At Home might have pulled the wool over your parents' eyes, and the You Around Your Friends might have your friends fooled. Maybe those Fake You's have it all together. But the Real You, well that's a different story.

My friends and I called it "The Mask." Like chameleons we'd change "who we were" depending on the company we were with. So after a night of partying, we'd wipe our faces clean, walk into our houses, and spin stories about the movie we had told our parents earlier we were going to. We'd walk into the classroom and pretend we were actually interested in Karl Marx (all the while not appearing too interested for fear that our classmates might accuse us of brownnosing). We'd go up to a group of girls at the mall and act like they were the prettiest little things we had ever seen and that our whole lives had merely been a cosmic leading up to this point and if they only gave us their numbers we would be true to them forever. And believe it or not, The Mask worked! Not all the time, but often enough. Our parents would be clueless, our teachers would give us extra credit, and once in a blue moon girls would actually give us their real numbers! The Mask. It worked pretty well.

However, The Mask came with a dark side. One lie led to more lies that led to more lies, which led to this tangled nest that made conversations with our parents really awkward. Which, to be honest, was sad. These were people who used to carry us on their shoulders and wipe our tears away; now, they felt like strangers. They became so annoying. Didn't they understand that the more they reached out to us, the more it made us push them away? Didn't they get that the closer they got to finding out the junk we were hiding, the more we became afraid of the loss of their approval? Of course, we never saw their invasions of our privacy for what they were—a display of love and concern. The fact is we loved them, too. Unfortunately, The Mask made feelings like that impossible.

At school, The Mask reared its dark side in the form of stress. Because we were pretending to be good students and good students got good grades (good students also studied, but, you see, we weren't really good students, were we?), we felt the burden of performance. We faked our way to the grade (because the grade was all that mattered, right?). We were forced to succeed; because if we failed, say, the test after acing all the quizzes, then our teachers would figure out we had been cheating all along. And if the teacher discovered the fact that we couldn't tell the difference between Karl Marx and Groucho Marx, our futures would end up in ashes like Groucho's cigar. So we crammed, we cheated, we got sick from the stress, and we got the grade (or maybe we didn't). But one thing was sure: We didn't learn a thing about Karl Marx. And at the end of the day, the only thing school really taught us was how to succeed by doing as little as possible.

At least, The Mask got us girls' numbers. Sometimes, those numbers even led to dates, *even* kisses. Unfortunately, The Mask could never deliver on the love we were really after. No amount of digits or kisses could give us that because love is different than that. Love is intimacy, which requires vulnerability. And The Mask was like the opposite of vulnerability. Think about it. How could the *real me* be loved when I wasn't being *myself*? As long as we hid behind The Mask, we could never be loved, and yet if we took it off ... What if they didn't like what they saw? What if they rejected us? That would be worse than never being loved at all. Safer to stick with The Mask, we decided. At least, we'd be protected.

And never be truly loved ...

Here's a novel question: Wouldn't life be better without The Mask?

Sure. But there's a problem, see. We hinted at it in the last study. It's the reason we put The Mask on in the first place.

Psalm 14 describes us pretty well. It says we have all turned and become corrupt. "There is none who does good, not even one." Romans 3:23 puts it this way: "All have sinned and fall short of the glory of God." Notice the word *all*. Last time I checked, *all* meant everyone. You and me included. We are *all* in the same boat. Notice also the word *sin*. What is sin exactly? Sin is basically this: choosing our way over God's way. And like it or not, we were born with this attitude. That's right, sin comes naturally to us. And these self-centered, me-first, want-it-now natures have led us up some seriously wrong mountains.

We've all done it. God says, "I know what's best for you." We say, "I'd rather be in charge, thanks." God says, "Honor your parents." We say, "But have you seen my parents?" God says, "Don't let other stuff be more important than Me." We say, "Yeah but if I don't get into State, my life will be over." Or, "But what will my friends think?" Or, "But I want to have sex now." Or, "But it's not hurting anybody."

I could go on, but I don't have to. I know that you know you're a mess.

Now, what you do with this knowledge is what matters. So here I want to spend a bit of time.

If you're like me, the first thing you do when you make a mess is you try to *clean it up*. This works sometimes. But if you have ever made a big mess, like my teenage friend did last week when he ran over a mailbox and dented his mother's Lexus, then cleaning it up is not so easy. In this case, if the mess is too big to make it go away, you go to Plan B: *you cover it up*. Just like I did this morning. See, every Wednesday the cleaning ladies come to our house (best money I ever spent!). But the thing is, with cleaning ladies, you have to "clean up" in order for them to *clean up*. There's irony there, I know. Now what happens Wednesday morning is I pick up all the clothes I've strewn about the floor and stuff them into the closet. That's what we do, isn't it? We stuff things. We hide them. I'm speaking broadly, but you and I spend a lot of time and energy concealing our messes from others, don't we? Erasing texts. Clearing our internet histories. Telling lies to cover up our lies. It's what we do. But sometimes, hiding doesn't work. We get busted, outed. What do we do then? *We blame.* It's not our fault. It's our screwed-up parents. It's our crazy teachers. It's peer pressure. It's the media. You know what's interesting? Way back, when Adam and Eve break the rules in Genesis, the first thing Adam does is blame Eve. Then, in the next breath, he *blames God* for making Eve! Then Eve, not to be outdone, goes and blames the serpent (see Genesis 3:12–13). Neither of them take responsibility. That would be ...

Well, that would be what God would want us to do. But we don't want to do what God wants us to do. Our self-centered, me-first, want-it-now natures want to get away with it and not have to face the consequences.

Because here's the rub: There are consequences to the messes we have made of our lives. And these consequences are severe. Eternal even. Romans 6:23 says "the wages of sin is death." Wages? Basically, wages are what we have "earned" by sinning. And what is it we have earned by sinning? It's pretty clear. It's *death.*

Did you know that according to God's original design we were meant to live forever? Sadly, we humans have chosen another path, and it doesn't lead to Mount Sheridan. It leads to hell. Adam and Eve's sin introduced death to the world. And ultimately, if something is not done, death is facing all of us forever.

This is the reality that the world has been facing ever since the beginning. And like big messes, we can try our best to clean it up, cover it up, or blame it away, but the truth is, in the end, my mess is on me. Just like your mess is on you.

Get this: We've got to own our mess. Why? Because an honest assessment is the only way to get at the truth, and it's part of what must happen if we ultimately want to become whole people. However, wholeness doesn't come with confession. You and I need a major do-over. And do-overs don't come cheap.

In fact, they cost Jesus everything.

Study 3

Paratrooper Jesus

Here's a question for you. Way back in the Garden of Eden, was everything good? Uh, yes. God made everything and said it was good, right? Not exactly. Wait. Are you telling me that God made something *not good*? Not exactly. It was more the lack of something. Read it for yourself. Genesis 2:18: "The LORD God said, 'It is not good for man to be alone'" (NIV 1984).

Think about it. God created stars, galaxies, planets, water, land, fish, birds, animals, and man, and all of it was good. But Adam was alone. And it was not good for Adam to be alone. Turns out the universe hinges on relationships. God needs them, and so do we. It's been that way since the beginning.

Hold on. God *needs* something? It's true. God needs relationship. In fact, His existence involves one. It's called "the Trinity." God, the Father; God, the Son; and God, the Holy Spirit. They all have the same nature but they are separate individuals, and they show up in different ways.

So does this mean that we are not whole unless we get married? No! Of course not. Think about Jesus. If there ever was a person who was the total package, it was Jesus. He was so full of life people swarmed around Him wherever He went. He didn't need a lady—in fact, He didn't need anybody, only His Father. As it turns out, the love of God is all any of us really need. *And Jesus came so we could experience God's love personally by being in a relationship with Him.*

But if that was the only reason Jesus came, Adam wouldn't have needed Eve, nor would God have wanted Adam and Eve to have children and grandchildren and great-grandchildren. The fact is, God wants people to have relationships with each other, too.

Get this: God made Eve both for Himself *and* for Adam. And for a moment everything was right in the universe. Scripture says, "The man and his wife were both naked and were not ashamed."[1]

Consider the symbolism. Adam and Eve were *naked*; there was nothing to hide; nothing to keep them from knowing each other completely. In other words, to use the previous lesson's terminology, *no Mask*.

God meant for us to live naked. Not bare-skinned, but shame-free. God intended us to be fully loved, fully accepted, and fully worthy just the way we are. So what happened? As the story goes, the serpent (Satan) planted the idea in Adam and Eve's heads that God should not be trusted. In a word, the serpent lied. He claimed that if a person gained the knowledge of good and evil (i.e., ate of the fruit), then he or she would be like God.[2] Not true. But Adam and Eve were fooled. They thought to themselves ... *Wow. To be like God ... that sounds nice.*

Long story short, Adam and Eve took the bait, and all at once the most awful thing in history happened: "The eyes of both were opened, and they knew that they were naked." Their reaction: "They sewed fig leaves together and made coverings for themselves."[3] You get it? They made the first masks in history. And let me tell you: it was *not* good.

Sin entered the world, and the world fell like dominos. Everything—every tree, every plant, every fish, every bird, every animal, and every person (you heard me, every girl and boy, all the way up to you and me)—got corrupted. Sin broke God's grand design. As a result, the world and every relationship in it would never be what it was meant to be.

Friends, that's a problem. Because of sin, you will never be the person God meant you to be, and neither will I. And like we discussed in the last study, what we do when we come face-to-face with this reality is we clean up, cover up, blame it away, and worse. *We feel shame.* Let me tell you, shame is the silent killer. And we come to its silent conclusion that life would be a whole lot better with a mask on as opposed to the alternative, which is to be exposed for the messes that we are.

Listen: *You and I cannot be the people God meant us to be.*

Now, if that was the end of the story, that would really *not be good*. Thank God, it's not. You see, from the moment sin corrupted the world, God went into action to make it new again. And ultimately that plan resulted in God sending His very own Son. Get this: *Jesus came on a mission—to make a way for us to get our Real Selves back.*

Who is this Real Self? Well, it's the mask-free you, the beautiful, one-of-a-kind person God had in mind before you were even born.

You see, God wasn't willing to let His creation go down without a fight. "For God so loved the world, that he gave his only Son, that whoever believes in him should not perish but have eternal life."[4] You and I didn't deserve this. We were the ones who turned our backs. And yet, "God did not send his Son into the world to condemn the world, but in order that the world might be saved through him."[5] It was a masterful move, one that only God could have done; and with it, He was able to change the cosmic equation forever.

What did He do? *The Message* translation puts it this way:

> ... everything of God finds its proper place in [Jesus] without crowding. Not only that, but all the broken and dislocated pieces of the universe—people and things, animals and atoms—get properly fixed and fit together in vibrant harmonies, all because of [Jesus'] death, his blood that poured down from the Cross.[6]

Because Jesus was the exact representation of God, He showed us what God is really like. And there's more. He did something we could not do: He lived a mess-free life. That's right. Jesus never sinned. Not once. But it wasn't Jesus' perfect life that rescued us. It was His death. Why?

There are two ways to answer that question. The first has to do with the Law. The second has to do with Love. Both are vitally important to understand. So lean in.

Here we go: way one. God is just, and so just like the universe must obey the laws He put in place, so must He. However, God put a provision in the law that a crime (sin) could be paid (atoned) for by something else, provided that the something else wasn't also guilty. That last part was the problem—*everyone was guilty*. So what God did (pre-Jesus) was develop a system where animals could be slaughtered in our place. (You can read a detailed account of how this was done in Leviticus 16.) It was messy and bloody and didn't entirely work since animals and humans are not the same. You get it? Jesus was human *and* perfect. He did not deserve to be punished. But when He died on the cross, God was able to count His punishment as payment for our crime. No one else in history could have done this for us, because no one in history, except Jesus, has been guilt-free.

Everything changes because of the cross.

Because Jesus died, we have legal standing with God. It's not that our crimes have gone away; it's that the payment for those crimes has been served in full. God *can't* punish us. Doing so would be punishing two people for the same crime. It's what our American legal system calls "double jeopardy," and *that* would be unfair. And as we said already, God is just; He cannot be unjust. If He was, He wouldn't be God.

So does this mean that everyone goes to heaven? No. It means that everyone *can* go to heaven. C.S. Lewis said this: "I willingly believe that the damned are, in one sense, successful, rebels to the end; that the doors of hell are locked on the inside."[7] What keeps people sentenced to hell is not God, but our refusal to accept what His Son has done for us.

Jesus did what only He could do. He paid for our sin. "For our sake he made him to be sin who knew no sin, that in him we might become the righteousness of God."[8] "He himself bore our sins in his body on the tree [the cross], that we might die to sin and live to righteousness."[9] "For Christ also suffered once for sins, the righteous for the unrighteous, that he might bring us to God."[10] Just three of many verses I could share with you to describe what some have called The Great Exchange. We deserved death, but Jesus died in our place, so now instead of dying, we can have what Jesus deserves: eternal life!

But why would Jesus do such a thing? That is equally important to understand, and harder.

Have you seen the movie *Finding Nemo?* I'm guessing you have. It's a story of a clownfish who disobeys his father's orders and, as a result, gets kidnapped by a dentist and doomed to be a present to the dentist's niece Darla, the fish killer. Well Marlin, Nemo's father, isn't willing to let that happen. He drops everything and races across the ocean to save his son. He survives a shark attack, exploding underwater mines, a trip to the bottom of the ocean, an encounter with a glowing anglerfish with death daggers for teeth, not to mention electrocution by a smack of jellyfish.

Well, news of the father's undaunted love spreads over the waves. Turtles tell a school of fish, who tell lobsters, who tell dolphins, who tell swordfish. "He'll stop at nothing until he finds his son," says one dolphin. "That's one dedicated father," replies another. Finally, the story reaches Nigel, a pelican, who just so happens to know Nemo's whereabouts. Fast as he can, Nigel flies to the dentist's office to tell Nemo the great news.

At first Nemo listens to the pelican's story with disbelief. "Sharks? That can't be my dad."

"You sure?" asks Nigel. "What was his name? Some kind of sport fish or something. Tuna. Trout."

"Marlin?" tries Nemo.

"That's it!" replies Nigel. "The little clownfish from the reef."

"It's my dad! He took on a shark!" cries Nemo.

"I heard he took on three," says Nigel.[11]

Well, friends, you have a Father who loves you infinitely more than even Marlin loved Nemo. And Marlin might have faced 4,800 shark teeth, but Jesus squared off against all the powers of darkness for you. And Marlin might have gone to the deepest part of the ocean for his son, but Jesus went to the depths of hell and back for you. And Marlin might have taken on the jellies, but Jesus took on the cross. He took the nails. He took on our mess, our shame. And just like Marlin stopped at nothing to get his son back, Jesus stopped at nothing until He rescued you.

Because of his love for his son, Marlin did whatever it took. In the same way, because of God's love for us, *Jesus did whatever it took to save us.* He was like a paratrooper. Risking His life, He went behind enemy lines to find you. And finding you, He put you on His back and fought off everything the evil one threw at Him to bring you home.

Scripture says "God shows his love for us in that while we were still sinners, Christ died for us."[12] "'I will be found by you,' declares the LORD, 'and will bring you back from captivity.'"[13] And how about this: "Greater love has no one than this, that someone lay down his life for his friends."[14] Who said it? Jesus said it, then *did it*.

He laid down His life not only because it had to be done but also because He loved you so much He refused to live without you.

Listen, you might not feel loveable, likeable, or deserving in the least, but that doesn't change God's love for you. From Genesis to Revelation, all of Scripture points to this one truth: *God loves you and He will stop at nothing until He gets you back.*

I love watching Nemo's face as the story of his father's love unfolds. It goes from disbelief, to shock, to awe, to acceptance. And you know what happens once Nemo believes? He swims straight to the filter—the spot of his greatest shame, the thing he is most afraid to face— and he goes for it. And this time he makes it through. I love that. The father's love transforms Nemo.

And the same thing can happen to you. Because of what Jesus did for you on the cross, there is now nothing standing between you, God, and the life you were meant to experience with Him.

What do I mean by life? I mean *life*—life here on earth, and life forever in heaven. You see, Jesus didn't stay dead. Three days later, God brought Him back to life. Not only that, God also gave Jesus authority *over* life and death. What does that mean? Well, it means that Jesus has the power to give life forever to other people. Do you get it? Because of Jesus, we can now live life forever with Him!

So what do you need to do to begin this relationship with God and receive this life you are meant to live?

That's what the next study is for.

---

[1] Genesis 2:25.

[2] Genesis 3:5.

[3] Genesis 3:7 (NIV 1984).

[4] John 3:16.

[5] John 3:17.

[6] Colossians 1:19–20 (*The Message*).

[7] C. S. Lewis, *The Problem of Pain* (New York, New York; Harper Collins, 1940) 130.

[8] 2 Corinthians 5:21.

[9] 1 Peter 2:24.

[10] 1 Peter 3:18.

[11] *Finding Nemo* (Pixar, 2003).

[12] Romans 5:8.

[13] Jeremiah 29:14 (NIV 1984). This is a promise God made more than five hundred years before the birth of Jesus!

[14] John 15:13.

Study 4

All-In

There's a great story that John Dickson tells in his book *Humilitas*. Back during the Depression three young guys got on a Detroit city bus and quickly tried to pick a fight with their fellow passenger, a man sitting by himself.

No matter how much they taunted him, he didn't respond. After a while, he stood up. He was ginormous. Still not speaking, he pulled out his business card and handed it to them as he coolly stepped off the bus.

The young guys looked at the card. It read, simply, *Joe Louis. Boxer*.

Why was that significant, you ask? Because as anyone back then would have known, the man they had just tried to pick a fight with was the heavyweight champion of the world. In fact, the International Boxing Research Organization calls him the greatest boxer of all time (by way of comparison, Muhammad Ali is second).[1]

All that to say, it's good to know who you're messing with before you start messing with him.

My friend Paul Barclay used to tell this story about buying his first car. He had been saving up money for a while, and finally, when he thought he had enough, he rode his bike down to Lloyd's Used Car Lot. His dad knew Lloyd, and Paul thought that the guy might give him a deal. Parking his bike against a fence, Paul started looking in windows.

"Hey," yelled a gnarled old car salesman. "Stop breathing on the merchandise."

"Sorry," said Paul. "I'm here to talk to Lloyd."

"You're talking to him," said Lloyd.

"I want to buy a car," said Paul.

Lloyd waved the statement off. "We'll get to that. Whose are you?"

"My name's Paul."

"No," said Lloyd, clearly irritated, "*Whose* are you?"

"I'm Paul," said Paul, clearly confused.

Paul said Lloyd got this look in his eye like he was about to hit him, "Who claims you, son?"

"My dad, John Barclay."

"Oh," said Lloyd, his face suddenly changing. "You're John's boy. Come right in."

That day, Paul Barclay drove out of that car lot having learned a big lesson: *Knowing* whose *you are makes all the difference in the world.*

John (the author of the Gospel) wrote this: "To all who did receive him [Jesus], who believed in his name, he gave the right to become children of God."[2]

When you receive Jesus by believing in Him, you receive all the rights, privileges, and responsibilities that come with being part of God's family. And the first *right* is in the verse we just read: You have *the right* to become a child of God. Once you accept it, no one can take it away from you. In Jesus, you have a Father who loves you and wants you to live forever with Him. Wow!

So what exactly does it mean to *believe*? Great question. The Merriam-Webster Dictionary defines *belief* as "a feeling of being sure that someone or something exists or that something is true." That's the dictionary answer. However, when Jesus said the word, He meant something closer to how E. Stanley Jones writes about it: "I once talked to General Smuts, premier of South Africa and the author of *Holism*. He called my attention to something I've never forgotten. He said the word 'belief' is literally 'by-lief' or 'by life.' Your belief is your life. And your life is your belief. You believe in a thing enough to act on it, to live it. So you are what you believe, and you believe what you are. Your deed is your creed. And your creed is your deed."[3] In other words, what you believe is what you stake your life on. By *believing in Jesus*, you are saying, "I stake my life on who Jesus says I am and who He says He is." In contrast, *believing in yourself* would mean you are defining your life based on who you say you are. *Believing in what others think about you* would mean that you are giving other people the privilege of defining you.

Well, guess what happens when you *believe* in Jesus. God claims you as His child. He adopts you into His family. As a result, you gain all the rights and privileges that come with the title. So when you step onto the used car lots of this world and someone asks, "Who claims you?" you can straighten up and say, "God." Now, I can't guarantee that saying something like that will get you that sweet car deal you're looking for, but when you stand at the gates of heaven and someone asks you the final exam question, *Whose are you*? You can tell that angel or whoever it is, "I'm God's." And the angel will ask you to prove it. And you can look that angel straight in the eye and say, "I've staked my life on Jesus and the fact He died for me." And all of the sudden the angel will change his tune, and say, just as Lloyd said to my friend Paul, "Come right in."

SharpTop Cove is one of Young Life's camp properties. If you have been to a Young Life camp then you know that these properties are not so much camps as they are resorts for teenagers. Well, SharpTop, situated in the deep green mountains of Georgia, is one of my favorites. And for a few summers, I brought friends of mine there for the best week of their lives.

There is never a dull moment and no shortage of fun at Young Life camp, and my friends and I took full advantage. For a week we zip-lined, mountain biked, rock climbed, and Frisbee golfed. Then came the afternoon we did "The Quantum Leap." Its colloquial name is "The Pamper Pole," for reasons you will soon understand. Forty feet high with a small two-by-two piece of plywood on top, it is, for lack of a better description, a telephone pole in the woods. All you have to do is climb these U-shaped screws to the top, stand on the tiny platform, and jump to a bell that is dangling from a rope about six feet away. From the ground, it doesn't look very hard. You're clipped into a rope the whole time, so if you fall the only thing you could lose is a little dignity.

No problem. Or so it feels like from the ground.

However, the view is quite different from on top. Up there, the pole is swaying, your knees are knocking, your heart is lodged in your trachea, and your stomach, well, let's just say they don't call it the Pamper Pole for nothing. Now remember, you're still harnessed in. The truth of the situation has not changed. But your experience of it has changed considerably.

Belief can change, too. From the ground, you can observe every part of the Quantum Leap. You can put on the harness, you can feel the rope, and based on the evidence, you can *believe* that the rope will hold you and the harness will not break. But that kind of belief is nothing like the kind of belief that's required by the person being asked to jump from the top of the Quantum Leap. *That* is belief. When a girl jumps from a platform forty feet in the air with only a rope standing between her and certain death, she is staking her entire life on the belief the rope is enough to hold her.

The same goes with believing in Jesus. They don't call it a leap of faith for nothing.

Let me tell you, in life, you are going to meet a lot of bench-warmer believers—folks who say they believe this and that about God. It will be tempting for you to join them on the bench and believe from the safety of the ground.

But the life Jesus wants for you is something drastically different. He's going to ask you to strap on the harness of faith and trust Him. It's that scary. And it's that amazing. *Face it. You can't have a real relationship with God from the ground.*

One summer, I took several high school friends of mine to British Columbia for a week of sea kayaking through the Princess Louisa Inlet. A yachting magazine had recently ranked the area the most beautiful place in the world. Baby seals, bald eagles, salmon the size of your arm—it was a once-in-a-lifetime kind of trip. And we got to live it for seven days.

The night before we returned to base camp, one of the guys and I stayed up late on the rocks to talk about what following Jesus was going to look like back at home. It was a great talk. Afterward, we noticed that the guides were all standing along the shore. They were throwing rocks in the water. (Guys do that.) But here was the crazy part. Everywhere the rocks landed, water would explode into light. Bioluminescence it's called. We had found ourselves watching one of the most incredible phenomena in the world: a dinoflagellate bloom. These tiny organisms react to movement by glowing. I asked a guide if it was safe to get in. He said he thought so. That was all we needed to hear. The next second, our shirts were on the shore and we had jumped in.

It was unreal, like swimming in your own laser lightshow. Every once in a while a fish would swim beneath our feet and light up the depths. (There is a scene in the movie *Life of Pi* when Pi finds himself in a dinoflagellate bloom and a whale leaps out of the water. That's what it was like!) I just had to wake up the others. They all had to experience this.

The boys were grumpy, but they came. At the shore, the guide explained the dinoflagellate phenomenon. I told the guys to follow me in. Two shrugged and said, "Wow, that's cool," then trudged back to their sleeping bags. One guy rolled up his pajamas and walked in up to his knees. Finally, two joined us. Man, did we have fun.

Later, one of the guides who went on our trip shared what he wrote in his journal about the night. His insights are great.

> I wanted to write you because I had this total God moment while I was reflecting on our trip. It has to do with the night of the bioluminescence ... I started to journal about that day and I got to the part of going to wake up the boys and tell them that they were about to experience one of the most amazing phenomena out there. We got to the shore's edge and told them that the dinoflagellates' bloom glows when it moves. As I was writing God opened my eyes to a bit of what it is like to get out of the boat and follow him. From afar the bio doesn't look that

impressive (from the shore), it is just a faint glow when you see someone swimming in it. For [the two that] decided to stay on shore, the night will not be that memorable and truthfully they didn't want to get out of their comfort zone of a dry warm sleeping bag to jump into the unknown of the water. [One] was more intrigued and decided to splash around just off the shore, and he enjoyed himself but jumped in real quick and got out. He noticed the bio glow more because he was able to move his feet in it. I think [he] will remember it but you could tell the difference between his experience and [that of the two who jumped in]. They went all the way in and when you are all the way in, the bio is sooooo much more amazing than when you see from shore. Those guys were oozing with joy and happiness as they truly did experience all the beauty. I just thought that this picture is a real picture of some of the struggles and truths of following Christ. From afar it can seem not exciting, a "have to" life ... yet when you get off the comforts of the shore and jump in head first you no longer want to be on the shore and the joy and beauty, and love of Christ fill you up. You discover that being in the deep ocean of a relationship with Jesus is exactly where you want to be.[3]

The thing about the Quantum Leap, swimming in bioluminescence, and following Jesus is this: You'll only know what it's really like after you take the risk. But also like the Quantum Leap, swimming with dinoflagellates, and Jesus: You don't have to fear. He'll catch you. All you have to do is leap. Come on, jump in! What are you waiting for?

---

[1] John Dickson, *Humilitas: a Lost Key to Life, Love, and Leadership*, (Grand Rapids, Michigan; Zondervan, 2011), 26–27.

[2] John 1:12.

[3] E. Stanley Jones, *The Word Became Flesh*, (Nashville, Tennessee; Abingdon Press, 2006), 48.

[3] Used by permission of Mathias Newell.

Study 5

The Answer To Life's Final Exam

The Gates of Hell, that's what folks called it. From the back of the Temple of Pan, the earth god, water gushed out of a gaping mouth at the base of the cliff. This was the place where pagan idol worshippers took their children and sacrificed them by tossing them into the turbulent current. If the cave swallowed the child, it meant that the parents' offering was considered "acceptable." If the child was swept downstream, then their offering was "rejected," and they'd have to sacrifice another child. Nice spot for a picnic, wouldn't you say?

Well, that's where Jesus took His friends. It's called Caesarea Philippi. I've been there. It's in northern Israel, near Lebanon, and today, it actually is a very nice place to have a picnic.

Back then, the area was overrun with hedonism and idol worship. No self-respecting Jew would have set foot in a place like this. No one except Jesus. He wasn't scared of anything. He was the man who earlier told His disciples, "Do not think that I have come to bring peace to the earth. I have not come to bring peace, but a sword."[1] Jesus came to destroy places like this. Pagan idols were like Lego blocks to Him. On the other hand, the disciples were freaking out. Not only were they trespassing in enemy territory, they had reached the heart of darkness. There was no protection from the Romans here. If their oppressors felt like making sacrifices of them, they'd be goners, sink *or* swim.

Little did they know Jesus was about to ask them the most important question of their lives...

Let's pick up the story from here. Matthew 16:13 says, "Now when Jesus came into the district of Caesarea Philippi, he asked his disciples, 'Who do people say that the Son of Man is?'" What's going on here? Why is Jesus asking His disciples about the rumors that are swirling around about Him? Was He suffering an identity crisis? Had He not been feeling the love? Had His approval ratings slipped?

What was Jesus up to?

The disciples had no clue how to answer. "John the Baptist?" tried one. "Elijah," attempted another. "Jeremiah," said a third. Stabs in the dark. Basically, the disciples were listing famous prophets, hoping one would be right.

It reminds me of the time my friend was leading a discussion in his cabin at a Young Life camp. He thought he'd start the discussion by tossing the guys a softball. He said, "So tell me, what's gray, has a bushy tail, and likes to eat nuts?" The guys looked at each other. Everyone's thinking squirrel. You could almost see the furry little mammal floating in the thought bubbles above their heads. But this was a small group of guys—no one wanted to be the first to speak. Finally, one boy worked up the nerve to answer. He said, "Well, to me, it sounds like a squirrel, but I'm gonna have to answer Jesus."

Ha! These fellas had been to enough "churchy" things to know that Jesus is the answer to most questions. (I guess you could say that my friend's softball of a question turned out to be a curve ball to these guys.)

Well, after Jesus listened to His disciples' I-don't-have-a-clue answers, you wouldn't have blamed Him if He had lost His temper and shouted, "Idiots!" But unlike my friend leading his cabin time, who, according to my sources, said something a little saltier than "Idiots!", Jesus kept His cool. He was Jesus after all. Instead of throwing down lightning bolts like Zeus (who also had a statue at Caesarea Philippi), Jesus lowered His voice and asked His disciples a follow-up question: "What about you? Who do *you* say I am?"

You get the sense the disciples were feeling intimidated. Here they were, standing outside the rushing water at the Gates of Hell with a guy who could control storms, walk on water, and raise the dead.

I imagine Phillip whispered to Andrew, "You think He's planning to throw us in to see who floats?"

Feeling vulnerable, Nathaniel ducked for cover behind James.

Suddenly, Simon cleared his throat, and the rest of the disciples took a collective sigh of relief. Among the disciples, Simon had become notorious for putting his foot in his mouth. If someone was getting tossed into the Gates of Hell, it was going to be him. "Maybe Jesus will throw out His back," whispered Andrew, Simon's brother. Simon was a big guy after all.

Phillip shushed him. He wanted to listen. They all did as Simon answered, "You are the Christ, the Son of the living God."

What? Did Simon just say what I think he just said? Jesus, the Messiah? He's been healing people, performing miracles, and talking about God as if He knows Him personally. But still. There's only going to be one Messiah in history, and you think a guy like that would choose to hang out with a bunch of misfits like us?

That's what the rest of the disciples were thinking.

At the moment, Jesus looked at Simon as if Simon was the only one there. He placed a hand on his shoulder. Up the hill, the Gates of Hell roared with turbulence. The air felt weighty around them. Jesus' lips parted, His eyes locked on Simon. The disciples held their breath.

"Blessed are you, Simon Bar-Jonah!" Jesus replied, His lips curling into a smile, "For flesh and blood has not revealed this to you, but my Father who is in heaven. And I tell you, you are Peter, and on this rock I will build my church, and the gates of hell shall not prevail against it."[2]

Doggone it, if Simon didn't answer Jesus right! Not only that, but he got a new name out of it.

Jesus and Simon/Peter turned toward their friends as understanding was beginning to filter from one disciple to the next. *They were at the Gates of Hell. Carved in these cliffs were upwards of one hundred deities.* And here was Jesus standing in the middle of them asking, "Who am I? Do you believe I'm only a man? Do you think of Me as just one of these hundred deities on the wall? Or do you believe that I am Lord over all of them?"

How you answer makes a difference.

In fact, two thousand years later, it still does.

Get this: On life's final exam there is one question: "Who do you say Jesus is?" Not who does your pastor say He is, or your Young Life leader, or the textbook you haven't read, or the History Channel, or your friend Bubba, for that matter. YOU. Who do *you* say He is? The question is personal. Why? Because Jesus demands a personal response. No one can take the final exam for you. And how you answer says everything God needs to know about who you claim to be and what you stake your life on.

There you have it: the answer to the question is Jesus is the Christ (the Savior of the world), the Son of the living God.

You mean you've made me read all this just to tell me the answer is that Jesus is the Son of God and He saved us from our sins? I could have guessed that. Well, good for you. But there's more, of course. A lot more. Jesus didn't go to hell and back so you could fill in a blank with His name. He went to hell and back so that by *knowing Him* you could become the person God created you to be in the first place. Do you get it? It's not just "knowing" the answer that matters. The key to LIFE is *knowing* the answer. There's a difference between knowledge and *knowledge*.

You know, you could read every book, watch every movie, interview every person who stormed the beaches of Normandy, and you would know a lot *about* D-Day. But no amount of information is the same as someone who actually *experienced* it. Those veterans *know* what it was like. They *lived* it.

And, using an example from the previous study, just like there is a difference between believing from the ground versus believing from the top of Quantum Leap, knowledge follows the same kind of logic. Knowledge requires personal investment. It just does.

I'll use me as an example. I'm a pretty wide-open guy. Folks usually have me figured out for better and worse after one conversation. I even keep my Facebook settings on Public. But as well as friends, strangers, and acquaintances know me, compared to my wife, they don't know me at all. That's what marriage is—intimacy, exposure, vulnerability, and *knowledge*.

How about you? Who knows you? Not the person you pretend to be, but you. The Real You. That might be hard to answer. A lot of times I can't say that I really know myself. And if you want to know the truth, there truly is only one person who *really knows me*, and it's not my wife. She's gotten closer than any other regular human being, but even she doesn't know all of me.

Only Jesus knows me like that. He knows me better than I know me!

Same with you.

Now, this might be the most important thing to understand, so pay attention: As much as God wants to know you—He wants you to know Him!

It was January, and I was sitting down in this comfy brown recliner chair that one of my Young Life guys had given me. It was my "quiet time" chair, the place where I read my Bible and prayed. That's what I was doing there that morning.

But this morning was different for some reason. A thought had come to me, a question actually. "Do I really *know* Jesus?" What I meant was would I recognize Him if He walked into the room? Could I pick Him out of a lineup? Did I know what His laugh sounded like? Did I know His smell? I suddenly realized that I had stumbled upon something pretty important. Was it possible to really *know* Jesus? You know, the Guy I kept inviting people to have a "personal relationship" with—was it possible to have a *personal* relationship with Him?

Don't get me wrong; I loved Him. I believed He died for my sins. But did I *know* Him? I definitely knew a lot of things *about* Him. But could I honestly say I had a *personal relationship* with Jesus?

That morning it hit me that one day, after I died, I was going to spend eternity with a person I wasn't sure I really knew. See, I was a Christian; I had been one for years. I even worked for Him! But as much as I knew about Him, I wasn't sure if I *knew Him* very well. Sure, I could tell you stories. I could recite to you verses by heart, but did I know Him deep down in mine?

So on a whim I decided to do something radical. It might not sound very radical, but let me tell you, it was for me. That morning, I read the Bible not for what I could get out of it—like an application or an encouragement for the day—but *to get to know Jesus*. For as long as it took, I would be like Sherlock Holmes. I'd search for clues, study Jesus' every move, and build a profile until I knew the Man.

But where to begin? I decided on the Gospel of Mark (it is the shortest of the gospels). Flipping to chapter 1, I read real slow.

A year-and-a-half and close to five hundred "quiet times" later, I finished. Finished what, the Bible? Nope, the Gospel of Mark. Sixteen chapters in five hundred hours. It was an incredible experience. I would read a bit, write down observations, questions, insights, musings. I'd give myself poetic license and imagine what it must have been like to be there. I'd read the passage from different points of view. From time to time, I'd go to a reference book to learn more about the time period or culture. But for the most part, I just read the words on the page. And while I did so, this crazy thing happened. I fell in love. It's true. By the end of chapter 1, I knew Jesus better than I did in the first ten years of following Him. By the middle of the second chapter I would have followed this guy to the ends of the earth. I kept reading. And the story just got better. And Jesus would do things that amazed me. And He'd do things that shocked me, frustrated me, and many times surprised me. And that's when it started getting interesting because Jesus changed from this weird figment of my imagination into a person that was truly different from me. Jesus became someone I could relate to and battle with and learn from and rely on. In a word, He became *real*.

I *knew* Him.

And I am still getting to *know* Him.

John has this awesome line at the end of his Gospel. He writes, "Now there are also many other things that Jesus did. Were every one of them to be written, I suppose that the world itself could not contain the books that would be written."[3] I love that. It will take us forever to know Jesus all the way. Maybe that's why He invites us to live with Him for eternity ...

There is more I could write, too. Instead, I'll leave you with a challenge: *Get to know Jesus.* Pick a Gospel. There are four to choose from: Matthew, Mark, Luke, and John. For thirty days, be Sherlock Holmes. Read the words not for what you can get out of it, but to get to know Jesus.

You know that question, *Do you know Jesus?* The answer He's hoping to hear from you is, "I do." You know that, right? I do. Think about it. "I do" is what people in love say to each other at a wedding ceremony. It's the kind of commitment Jesus is making to you.

---

[1] Matthew 10:34.
[2] Matthew 16:17–18.
[3] John 21:25.

Study 6

The Get-To Life

If you had to pick the one thing Young Life is most known for, it would be camp. My friend and former United States Field Director for Young Life, Ty Saltzgiver, defines Young Life camp as "an extravagant resort in the middle of God's extravagant creation to proclaim to kids God's extravagant love for us in Jesus Christ." Key word: *extravagant*. Almost seventy years ago Jim Rayburn, the founder of Young Life, put it this way: "Who started this idea that Christians oughta have the seat of their pants in patches, or that we oughta have camps in tents? We talk about the King of kings; let's act like He's the one in charge! He's the one we represent! We're going to have the classiest camps in the country."[1]

In other words, the point of Young Life camp is to give the folks who come the clearest picture of the God who loves them and the life He wants them to live. Now what we mean by life is not the zip-lines or the Pamper Poles or the over-the-top desserts. What we mean is that at Young Life camp, Jesus is the center. Everything at camp points to Jesus. The people who serve the guests, the rides, the meetings, the leaders ... everything and everyone points to one thing: Jesus loves you.

Well, along those lines, one of the first things you hear when you go to Young Life camp is that *there are no rules*. What? That's right. You heard me. *No rules* (which is usually followed by the addendum: *However, we do have a few strong suggestions* ... I love that line).

Now, I'm not sure if the founders of Young Life camping knew this, but that no rules thing actually comes from Scripture. Jesus said it. In fact, of all the things Jesus talked about, freedom was the thing that made the religious leaders of the time the most uncomfortable. One time Jesus said, "If the Son sets you free, you will be free indeed."[2] You know how the religious leaders reacted? They picked up stones to kill him![3]

I think adults are afraid to tell you about this because like the religious leaders they're afraid about what you'll do with the freedom Christ offers. (And maybe they are right to be afraid.) But the bottom line is that there is total freedom when it comes to Jesus. Freedom for what, you might ask? Well, *in Christ, you are completely free to become the Real You.*

Now, being the Real You is not that easy. We've got these masks. We face these temptations. And worst of all, we have these self-centered, me-first, want-it-now natures that keep fooling us into doing what's not good for us. The truth is we get fooled all the time into feeling, thinking, and doing stuff that our Real You's would *never* want us to feel, think, or do. I speak from experience. In addition, although Jesus gives us freedom *to become* ourselves, He doesn't entirely give us freedom *from the consequences* of our choices—which is why following "a few strong suggestions" might help us grow into the persons God is shaping us into.

Haiti is a country that has been ravaged by corruption, bad government, extreme poverty, and natural disasters. A few years ago, my wife and I went there on a mission trip. We were met at the airport by François and his machine gun. A little unnerving to say the least. We learned that this was normal behavior in Haiti, which didn't make us feel any better. Two hours later, our bus pulled into base camp. It resembled a prison compound: cement walls twelve feet high with barbed wire strung around the top. The only thing missing was the jumpsuits. After "settling in," we divvied up jobs for the week. Lia was on the medical team, she being a doctor. I, having no skills, was given a pickax. Some mission group from the past had poured the foundation to a building that ended up being built elsewhere, and it was our job to remove it. Great. I was already feeling like a prisoner; now it was official. "I can't believe we have to do this," I groaned to my friend, Michael, who sells pharmaceuticals for a living (a.k.a. no skills). Michael nodded and put his arm around me. He had this strange smile on his face. "You got it all wrong, Ned. We don't *have to* do this; we *get to* do this." Michael took a few steps, raised his pickax over his head and swung it into the ground. "Into the ground" is an overstatement. It *pinged off the ground*. The ground went nowhere. He looked at me, laughed, and swung again.

I watched in awe. Here we were in the middle of the poorest country in the Western Hemisphere, surrounded by walls and machine guns, asked to do manual labor—and we had paid to come. This was what my wife and I had chosen to do for vacation. No one forced us to do this. We didn't *have to* be here. This was something we *got to do*.

I walked a few steps to the right of Michael (who swung a little wild) and plunged my ax toward the ground. *Ping.* A tiny flake of concrete flipped off the earth like a quarter toss. I kicked the teenie weenie chunk to the side. "I get to do this," I whispered, lifting my pickax high. "We get to do this," I said, putting every ounce of energy into the movement. *Ping.*

Who would have thought that fifty feet of concrete would change my life forever? I never had so much fun. The harder it got, the more joy it gave me. It was crazy. It was amazing. You know what it was? It was *real life.* John Bunyan, the author of the book *The Pilgrim's Progress*, is reported to have said: "You have not lived today until you have done something for someone who can never repay you." I experienced it that week in Haiti. But it was deeper than mere service. In the process, I realized that *the life Christ invites us to have is a "get-to," not a "have-to," life.*

Get this, my friends. I don't *have to* pray to be a good Christian. I *get to* pray because I want to spend time with Jesus. I don't *have to give money to the poor* to chalk up brownie points in heaven. I *get to* give my money away because I have realized that everything I have is all a gift to me in the first place. I don't *have to* go to church. I *get to* worship Jesus with my friends who *get to* worship Him, too. That's the life! No rules, total freedom.

So I don't *have to* quit doing drugs to be a Christian. I *get to* quit because I know Jesus lives in me and I want His house to be healthy. I don't *have to* drink alcohol to feel cool. I *get to* be myself because being yourself is cool. I don't *have to* wait to have sex before marriage. I *get to* give that gift to my wife. I *get to* wait so I can go into marriage with no baggage. And if I've had sex before, I *get to* be forgiven and become a virgin from this moment forward. I don't *have to* pretend I'm perfect. I *get to* do what's right without the worry of what happens when I screw up. I don't *have to* do good for Jesus to like me; I *get to* do good because I want to do what Jesus likes. As it turns out, what Jesus likes, I like, too!

A friend of mine went to law school and never once looked at his grades. It's true. My friend *never looked at his grades*. He just did his work and that was that. Why? Well, the way he put it was, "I didn't go to law school to get grades. I went to law school to learn." In his opinion, all grades did was stress people out. He figured someone would eventually tell him if he was failing. Well, my friend didn't fail. He finished near the top of his class.

That, my friends, is a picture of the *Get-To Life*.

But there are some things I *have to* do, right? Like brush my teeth. I have to do that. (No, you don't. You can totally follow Jesus with no teeth. My friend Lucy does it every day.) *But I don't want my teeth to rot,* you say. Well then, you better brush your teeth. In the Get-To Life, our choices still have consequences. And what we do with the freedom we have says a lot about what we believe. So, in your freedom, if you stop brushing your teeth and taking showers, then what you are saying is, "I am a slob." And if, in your freedom, you only eat potato chips, you will probably die of a heart attack when you're thirty. (And if you think that is what I'm saying by freedom, then I'd recommend reading this book over again.)

Jesus gave you freedom because He wants you to be *you*. Jesus came, He died, and He rose again so you could live the life you were made to live: a life in relationship with the God who knows you better than you even know yourself *because the greatest thing we get to do is get to know Him!*

On Moses 120th birthday, he stood up before the people he had been leading the last forty years and gave his last speech. Probably an important speech to listen to, wouldn't you say? Well, this is what he said:

> I set before you today life and prosperity, death and destruction. For I command you today to love the LORD your God, to walk in his ways, and to keep his commands ... then you will live ...

> But if your heart turns away and you are not obedient, and if you are drawn away to bow down to other gods and worship them, I declare to you this day that you will certainly be destroyed ...
>
> ... I have set before you life and death, blessings and curses. Now choose life, so that you and your children may live and that you may love the LORD your God, listen to his voice, and hold fast to him. For the LORD is your life ...[4]

Moses said God had given us a choice. Life or death. Love the Lord, walk in His ways, keep His commands ... basically, stake your life on Jesus and get to know Him, fall in love with Him, follow Him, become like Him—and *you will live.* But if you say "my way or the highway," and "I'll do whatever my self-centered, me-first, want-it-now self wants"—then, you'll end up where that road leads: *death*. Friends, don't choose death. CHOOSE LIFE! Love God, listen to Him, do what He says.

The LORD is your life and following Him leads you there!

Do you get it? From the moment God created life, He wanted His creation to experience it fully with Him. But He had this size problem, so He sent His Son so that His creation would know what He was like. But there were other problems, too; particularly, this problem called sin. It was a killer. It killed relationships. It killed souls. And it sentenced His creation to death forever. This was not acceptable to God. So He asked His Son Jesus to do the unthinkable: to pay the penalty of sin with His own blood. And that was exactly what Jesus did. He died on the cross to pay our debt in full. But Jesus didn't stay dead. God brought Him back to life. Not only that, God gave Him the power to give life to all of those who staked their lives on what Jesus did for them.

How do we do stake our lives on Jesus? We jump off the Pamper Pole by putting all of what we know of ourselves into all of what we know of God and trust that He is enough. And when we do this, we discover that we don't lose our freedom; instead, we experience freedom like we've never experienced it before!

Not only that, we discover that Jesus is now offering us the opportunity of a lifetime—to become the person God, from the beginning, meant for us to be. How do we become this person? We get to know Jesus. The more we get to know Him, the more we fall in love with Him. And the more we fall in love with Him, the more we'll follow Him. And the more we follow Him, the more we'll become like Him. And the more we become like Him, the more we become ourselves—our Real Selves.

There you have it. The answer. In one word, Jesus. Get to know Him, and let Him know you as well. Give Him full access to your heart. When you do, He'll transform your life from the inside out. Together, you will pass every test this world will throw at you. And at the end of your life, He will escort you into His home in heaven, where He has been planning an everlasting graduation party better than any party you have ever been to or could even imagine.

---

[1] Jim Rayburn, quoted by John Miller in an interview with Char Meredith for her book *It's A Sin to Bore a Kid* (Waco, Texas: Word Books, 1978).

[2] John 8:36.

[3] See John 8:59.

[4] Deuteronomy 30:15–20, (NIV 1984).

About the Author

Ned Erickson lives in Winston-Salem, North Carolina, with his wife, two kids, two dogs, six chickens, three hamsters, one turtle, and a fish. He is the author of *Falling Into Love* as well as the novel *Clay*, and has worked for Young Life for many years in a variety of roles. For more information visit his website: www.nederickson.com. Ned can be reached through the publisher at ran@whitecapsmedia.com.

Colophon

Book designed by Randolph McMann for Whitecaps Media

Main body composed in Chaparral Pro Regular 10.5/15. Chaparral Pro was created by Adobe designer Carol Twombly

Cover designed by Stephanie W. Dicken

426 Series editor: Kit Sublett

Be sure to visit
whitecapsmedia.com
for more
426 Series Bible studies
and the Study Guide
for this book

www.ingramcontent.com/pod-product-compliance
Ingram Content Group UK Ltd.
Pitfield, Milton Keynes, MK11 3LW, UK
UKHW021322180426
11947UKWH00017B/1390